Original title:
The Winter Light

Author: Paula Raudsepp
ISBN HARDBACK: 978-9916-79-465-4
ISBN PAPERBACK: 978-9916-79-466-1
ISBN EBOOK: 978-9916-79-467-8

Harbingers of Warmth

Soft whispers of spring, flowers in bloom,
Gentle sunbeams chase away the gloom.
Birds sing sweetly in vibrant trees,
Life awakens with a fragrant breeze.

Golden rays spread across the land,
Nature rejoices, a tender hand.
Promises of joy in every heart,
A brand new season, a fresh, new start.

Journey through a Glistening World

Crystal paths beneath our feet,
Starlit skies, a wondrous feat.
Every step, a spark of light,
Guiding us through the velvet night.

Whispers of magic fill the air,
Adventure beckons everywhere.
With each turn, a tale unfolds,
In this glistening world, our dreams hold.

Spangles of Daylight

Morning breaks with colors bright,
A canvas painted in pure light.
Every shadow fades away,
As spangles dance, welcoming the day.

Nature sighs in soft delight,
Embracing warmth, the world ignites.
Moments captured in radiant beams,
Life awakens, fulfilling dreams.

Illumination Amidst Ice

Frozen landscapes glimmer and shine,
Fractured light through branches entwine.
A stillness holds the winter air,
Beauty found in the cold's soft glare.

Glistening crystals on every tree,
Nature's artwork, wild and free.
In the silence, warmth does creep,
Illumination in the quiet deep.

Moonlight on the Snowdrift

Moonlight glimmers on white shrouds,
Whispers soft beneath the clouds.
A silver path through undisturbed,
Winter’s grace is gently curbed.

Starlight dances, flickers bright,
Casting shadows, pure delight.
Footprints vanish, secrets blend,
In this stillness, time suspend.

Branches bow with frosted wear,
Nature holds its breath in prayer.
Silent echoes meet the night,
Wrapped in blankets, cold and light.

Radiance in the Depths

In the ocean's heart, unseen,
Waves of color, deep and green.
Life pulsates in cyclical dance,
In the darkness, things enhance.

Glowing corals weave their thread,
In quiet waters, beauty spread.
Creatures drift in gentle sway,
Where the sun can't find its way.

Murky shadows, secrets keep,
As the currents lull to sleep.
Ancient songs of lost debris,
In the depths, they still are free.

Flickers of Dusk

Amber hues burn in the sky,
Daylight waves a slow goodbye.
Crisp and cool, the evening sighs,
Stars awaken with sleepy eyes.

Whispers dance on the evening breeze,
Rustling leaves in twilight's tease.
Shadows lengthen, embers glow,
Softly calling as night flows.

Silhouettes of trees stand still,
As the world begins to chill.
Laughter fades to gentle hum,
In the dusk, our hearts become.

Echoes of a Quiet Hearth

Flames flicker, a warm embrace,
Stories linger in this place.
Cinders glow with memories bright,
Hushed and held within the night.

Embers crackle, laughter sings,
As the hearth's warmth softly clings.
Time slows down, a sacred space,
Where love finds a gentle trace.

Beneath the mantle, shadows play,
Whispering secrets of the day.
In this circle, spirits weave,
Echoes of what we believe.

Starlit Quietude

In the hush of night so deep,
Stars above begin to weep.
Whispers float on gentle air,
Dreams unfold without a care.

Moonlight dances on the stream,
Casting spells that softly gleam.
Crickets chirp their lullaby,
As fireflies begin to fly.

In this peace, the world stands still,
Echoes linger, hearts will fill.
Every breath a notes sweet sound,
In starlit quietude, we're found.

Warmth Within the Cold

Snowflakes fall like whispered dreams,
Chill surrounds, but joy redeems.
By the fire, stories weave,
In the warmth, we dare believe.

Cocoa mugs in hands we hold,
Laughter shared against the cold.
Footprints trace a path of cheer,
In this moment, all is clear.

Winter's grasp may try its best,
Yet here together, we find rest.
Hearts ignited, spirits bold,
Discover warmth within the cold.

Leaps of Dappled Light

Through the leaves, the sun does play,
Casting shadows on the way.
Dappled light on forest floor,
Whispers beckon, hearts explore.

Every rustle, every sound,
Nature's magic all around.
Breezes swirl with laughter's song,
In this place, we all belong.

Tiny creatures dance in beams,
Living out their wildest dreams.
Moments fleeting, yet so bright,
Find your joy in leaps of light.

Traces of Aurora's Wing

In the twilight, colors blend,
Nature's canvas knows no end.
Auroras stretch across the sky,
Whispering secrets as they fly.

Fleeting glimpses, soft and grand,
Traces left by magic’s hand.
Stars align in cosmic dance,
Inviting all to take a chance.

Hearts uplifted, spirits sing,
Chasing dreams on colored wing.
Nature’s brush paints night’s embrace,
In the sky, we find our place.

Crystal Hues

In the dawn's soft light,
Shimmering crystals gleam,
Nature's gems on display,
Awakening the dream.

Whispers of the wind,
Dance through emerald leaves,
Each hue tells a tale,
Of the magic it weaves.

Blue skies hold the promise,
Of adventures anew,
Colors blend and swirl,
In a vibrant view.

Morning dew like diamonds,
On the grass so green,
A canvas of dreams,
In every serene scene.

As day turns to night,
Stars begin to play,
Crystal hues of twilight,
Guide us on our way.

Fragments of Cold Sun

Winter's touch, so crisp,
Carves the air with grace,
Fragments of a cold sun,
Warmth we still chase.

Biting winds sing low,
Through the barren trees,
Silent echoes linger,
Carried by the breeze.

Snowflakes gently fall,
Like whispers from the sky,
Each a fleeting moment,
As time drifts by.

Footprints in the snow,
Tell of lives once shared,
In this frozen kingdom,
Memories declared.

As twilight descends,
The world holds its breath,
In fragments of cold sun,
Life and beauty bequeath.

Frost-Kissed Serenity

Morning breaks in silver,
On the frosted ground,
Nature's soft embrace,
In silence we are found.

Gentle whispers float,
Through the chilly air,
Healing tunes of winter,
Follow without care.

Trees adorned in white,
Stand in regal pose,
Guardians of the stillness,
In their silent throes.

Footsteps soft and light,
Leave no trace behind,
Each moment a treasure,
In the peace we find.

As twilight casts a glow,
Over fields of frost,
Frost-kissed serenity,
A beauty never lost.

Luminous Frost

Moonlight spills like magic,
On the sleeping earth,
Luminous frost glimmers,
In winter's quiet birth.

Stars twinkle above,
In the velvet night,
Guiding us through shadows,
With their silver light.

Every crystal fragment,
Glows with a soft sheen,
Creating a wonder,
In this evening dream.

Whispers of the night,
Flow through icy streams,
Inviting us to wander,
In the realm of dreams.

As dawn breaks anew,
And the frost starts to fade,
Luminous memories linger,
In the light that cascades.

Shadows Catching Light

In the twilight's soft embrace,
Shadows stretch and twist with grace.
Sunset drapes the world in gold,
Whispers of secrets yet untold.

Leaves dance lightly to the ground,
Where the silent hopes are found.
A fluttering moment, captured bright,
As shadows chase the fading light.

Reflections on Icy Waters

Beneath the moon's watchful gaze,
Icy waters hold a haze.
Ripples whisper tales of old,
In mirrored depths, the night unfolds.

Stars twinkle on the frozen glass,
As time drifts gently, slow to pass.
Each reflection a fleeting sigh,
Caught between earth and sky.

Gentle Glimmers of Solitude

In quiet corners, peace resides,
Where gentle glimmers softly slide.
A single candle flickers low,
Casting dreams in warm, sweet glow.

Thoughts drift like feathers on the breeze,
Finding solace, hearts at ease.
In solitude's embrace, we find,
The softest whispers of the mind.

A Dance of Crystal Beams

Morning sunlight breaks the dawn,
Crystal beams like diamonds drawn.
Colors swirl in joyous flight,
A ballet crafted in the light.

Nature waltzes, branches sway,
As dawn unfolds a brand new day.
In the shimmer, bright and bold,
Life's cherished moments, pure as gold.

Softly Burning Bright

In the quiet of the night,
Flames dance, a soft delight.
Whispers of warmth and cheer,
Holding us, drawing near.

Embers crackle, softly sing,
A tender warmth they bring.
In shadows, stories play,
Lighting up the darkest way.

Dreams flicker in the glow,
Paths revealed, secrets flow.
Each spark, a wish so sweet,
In the glow, our hearts meet.

Moments linger, time is still,
Wrapped within this gentle thrill.
Together we find our light,
In the softly burning bright.

Luminous Guard of the Hearth

Gathered ‘round the fire's grace,
Warmth and love in this space.
A circle formed, bonds we share,
In the glow, we feel the care.

Crisp air outside, still and cold,
Within, the stories unfold.
Guarded by its shining core,
Hearts are safe forevermore.

Flames that leap, a watchful eye,
Luminous sparks against the sky.
Guiding dreams with every light,
Faith and hope burn ever bright.

As shadows dance, we sing our song,
A harmony that feels so strong.
In the hearth, our lives entwined,
Luminous guard, love aligned.

Expanse of Twilight's Glow

The sun dips low, a soft retreat,
Twilight stretches, calm and sweet.
Colors blend in gentle hue,
A canvas drawn of deepening blue.

Stars awaken, twinkling bright,
Filling the canvas with soft light.
Whispers carried on the breeze,
In this peace, the spirit frees.

Moonlight bathes the world in grace,
Each shadow finds its sacred place.
In the expanse, our dreams take flight,
Guided by the twilight's light.

Moments linger, quiet, pure,
In this stillness, we endure.
Embraced by night, cradled high,
Underneath the vast, starlit sky.

Celestial Lullaby

Close your eyes, my dear one, near,
Listen closely, the sounds are clear.
A lullaby from stars above,
Sung gently, wrapped in love.

Moonbeams weave a silver thread,
Cradling dreams upon your bed.
In the night's sweet, soft embrace,
Feel the warmth of this safe space.

Galaxies spin in perfect time,
Each heartbeat, a whispered rhyme.
Close your eyes, let worries fade,
In dreams, your spirit can cascade.

As the night wraps all in grace,
Lullabies in endless space.
Sleep, my darling, drift away,
To the stars where wishes play.

Frosted Glimmers

In the hush of dawn's first light,
Frosted whispers gleam so bright.
Nature's crystals dance and sway,
Capturing magic in their play.

Every leaf a diamond's tale,
Woven glimmers on the trail.
Silence blankets, pure and deep,
In the cold, the world will sleep.

Moments frozen in the air,
Glimmers twinkle everywhere.
Children laugh with pure delight,
Snowflakes twirl in morning light.

Branches draped in silver lace,
The quiet charm, a soft embrace.
Winter's breath, a gentle song,
In this realm, we all belong.

As the sun begins to rise,
Painting skies with softest sighs.
Frosted glimmers fade away,
But the memories, here to stay.

Shimmers of Serenity

Beneath the quiet of the moon,
Shimmers glow in still attune.
Nature rests in softest hush,
In the night all fears do crush.

Stars reflect on waters calm,
Serenity, our hearts' sweet balm.
Whispers float upon the breeze,
Carrying dreams through swaying trees.

Gentle waves kiss sandy shores,
Soft as peace that life restores.
In this moment, time stands still,
Wrapped in warmth, we feel the thrill.

As the night unfolds its grace,
Each shimmer holds a soft embrace.
In the stillness, hearts can mend,
Finding solace, time won't end.

Morning light will soon break free,
Chasing shadows, setting we.
Yet in dreams, we will return,
To the shimmers, where we yearn.

Chilled Radiance

With the dawn, a crisp surprise,
Chilled radiance fills the skies.
Ice-clad branches, nature's art,
Winter's breath warms every heart.

Every flake a tale unspoken,
In the silence, bonds unbroken.
Glistening on the frozen ground,
Magic whispers all around.

Sunlight filters through the trees,
Golden light dances with the breeze.
In the stillness, calm and bright,
Chilled radiance brings pure delight.

Children's laughter fills the air,
Snowman building, joyful flair.
Every smile, a spark divine,
In this chilly, bright sunshine.

As the day begins to wane,
Chilled radiance will remain.
In our hearts, we know the glow,
Of love's warmth in winter's show.

Brilliance in the Snow

Brilliance kisses every flake,
Painting white on every lake.
Snowflakes twirl like dreams in flight,
Lending magic to the night.

Every path a canvas pure,
Nature's art, so rich and sure.
With each step, the silence grows,
Wrapped in warmth as the stillness flows.

Winter's breath, a gentle tune,
Underneath the silver moon.
Every heartbeat echoes slow,
In the brilliance of the snow.

Through the woods, a spark will guide,
Whispers echo, love and pride.
In this wonderland we roam,
Finding peace, we feel at home.

As the evening shadows creep,
In our hearts, the memories keep.
Brilliance lingers, soft and low,
In our dreams, we dance with snow.

Shimmering in the Arctic Cycles

Whispers of ice in the pale blue night,
Stars dance above, a wondrous sight.
Snowflakes twirl, in a frosty breeze,
Nature's art, with such gentle ease.

Eagles soar through the crystalline air,
Silence enchants, beyond compare.
The world, a canvas, painted in white,
In the Arctic cycles, pure delight.

Each heartbeat echoes, the icebergs gleam,
Reflections shimmer, like a frozen dream.
With every sunset, a soft embrace,
In this tranquil land, we find our place.

The glacial paths whisper tales of old,
Stories of winter, timeless and bold.
Under the auroras, a mystical show,
In shimmering colors, the spirits glow.

Lost in the wonder, we breathe in deep,
Guardians of secrets that nature keeps.
In the Arctic's heart, forever we'll roam,
Across this vast, enchanting home.

The Luster of Iced Over Dreams

Beneath the frost, where shadows play,
Lies the magic of night and day.
Iced over visions, softly confined,
Whispers of hopes, forever enshrined.

Moonlight glimmers on a frozen lake,
Silent reflections, the heart will wake.
In this stillness, dreams come alive,
In the luster of night, we thrive.

Jack Frost kisses the windowpane,
Each frosty breath, a soft refrain.
The world spins gently in silver and blue,
Crafting a tapestry, old yet new.

With every heartbeat, the icy air calls,
A song of enchantment beneath starlit halls.
Through craggy peaks and valleys so deep,
The luster of dreams sends us to sleep.

Awake in the dawn, as the sun bows low,
The icy grip melts, yet memories flow.
In the warmth of day, our visions soar,
The luster of dreams forever to explore.

Luminescent Stillness

In the aurora's dance, the night stands still,
Colors of wonder, a joyful thrill.
Stars twinkle softly in the vast expanse,
A moment suspended, lost in a trance.

The air is crisp, with a chill so sweet,
Nature's quiet pulse, a rhythmic beat.
Snow blankets whispers of stories untold,
Under the cosmos, a beauty bold.

Frost-kissed branches glint like diamonds rare,
In this silence, we find solace there.
The world feels sacred, wrapped in the glow,
Of luminescent stillness, a soft ebb and flow.

Each breath we take, a crystal delight,
The stars bear witness to the tranquil night.
Within this magic, our spirits ignite,
In the heart of stillness, everything feels right.

When morning breaks, with its golden hue,
A legacy lingers, fresh and new.
But in our hearts, we hold the thrill,
Of luminescent stillness, the night stands still.

Light Beyond the Frost

Morning light creeps above the trees,
Melting away shadows with gentle ease.
Frost clings softly to the earth below,
A quiet promise, the sun will show.

Golden rays pierce the frosty veil,
Illuminating paths, a soothing trail.
In the crisp air, a new day begins,
Hope rises gently, like a song that sings.

Birds take flight on this wondrous morn,
Bound by the light, the dark is worn.
Each fluttering wing, a tale unfolds,
Of journeys awaiting, of dreams retold.

In the dance of seasons, a circle of life,
Frost turns to warmth, joy conquers strife.
With every sunrise, horizons expand,
Lighting the world, a delicate hand.

So let us wander where light breaks through,
Beyond the frost, where the heart feels true.
In this sacred moment, let love be sought,
For life finds its meaning in the light we fought.

Flickers of Hope and Chill

In the heart of a winter's night,
Flickers of warmth take flight.
Soft whispers through the trees,
Hope dances on the breeze.

Moonlight bathes the snowy ground,
A glimmer where dreams are found.
In shadows, courage takes its stand,
A silent plea, a gentle hand.

Stars above begin to shine,
Each twinkle a sacred sign.
The chill may bite, the winds may wail,
But hope, like fire, will not pale.

In the distance, a song of old,
Flickers of stories yet untold.
With every heartbeat, we transcend,
Embracing light, as dark days end.

So through the frost, we journey on,
In flickers, life will be reborn.
Each step, a promise, soft and clear,
Flickers of hope will persevere.

Gleaming Solitude

In a forest deep and still,
Where whispers hide and shadows fill,
Solitude shines, a gem so rare,
In the quiet, I lay bare.

The leaves fall slow, a gentle sigh,
Beneath the vast and open sky.
A single ray breaks through the grey,
Gleaming paths where dreams may play.

Each heartbeat echoes soft and low,
In this world, the agony slow.
But here, within the silent grace,
I find my truth in this embrace.

Time stands still, the moment grand,
With every breath, I understand.
In solitude, I bloom and grow,
Gleaming love I've come to know.

So let the world drift far away,
In solace, I choose to stay.
A gleaming heart, a mind at ease,
In solitude, I find my peace.

An Illumination in Silence

In the stillness, whispers fade,
An illumination softly laid.
Light dances on the edge of dreams,
Shimmering in tranquil streams.

Silence wraps the world so tight,
Moments glow in gentle light.
Each breath a flicker of the soul,
In quietude, we become whole.

Stars above begin to gleam,
Awash in the hush, we dream.
In this calm, we hear the call,
An illumination, a guiding thrall.

Soft echoes brush against the ear,
In silence, truths become so clear.
The heart beats louder, steady and strong,
In the less, our spirits belong.

So let the silence take its hold,
An illumination of stories told.
In each flicker, the night weaves tight,
A tapestry spun in the quiet light.

Radiant Silence of Crystal Air

In the morning's gentle dawn,
The world awakens, crisp and drawn.
Each breath a note, a whisper sweet,
Radiant silence with every beat.

Crystal air fills the hollow space,
Each moment slows, a tender grace.
Sunlight spills like liquid gold,
In silence, nature's beauty unfolds.

Through the veils of misty light,
The heart beats strong, dispelling night.
In emerald leaves, a soft refrain,
Whispers of joy that break the chain.

This radiant peace, a sacred song,
In stillness, we remember where we belong.
Harmony sings in vibrant hues,
In crystal air, we find our muse.

So let the silence gently stay,
As dawn breaks bright, lighting the way.
In radiant calm, our spirits soar,
In crystal air, forevermore.

Snowbound Brilliance

In silence deep, the snowflakes fall,
A blanket soft, embracing all.
The world transformed, a gleaming sight,
Each crystal spark, a twinkling light.

Beneath the hush, the dreams take flight,
Whispers dance in the cool moonlight.
Branches bow with winter's weight,
Nature sleeps, it's not too late.

Footprints traced in the frosty glow,
Children's laughter, sweet and low.
A glimmering path where shadows play,
In winter's arms, the heart will stay.

Resilience shines in each cold gust,
In frozen earth, we place our trust.
For soon the bloom will break the ground,
In snowbound brilliance, beauty found.

So cherish now this frozen grace,
In every flake, a warm embrace.
The magic swirls with every breath,
In winter's realm, we find our depth.

Icicle Dreams

Hanging low from eaves so high,
Icicles gleam against the sky.
Sharp and clear, like crystal tears,
Holding tight to winter's fears.

Drifting thoughts in cold night air,
Shimmering dreams, both bright and rare.
Each drip a story, frozen fast,
Moments caught, forever cast.

Icicles sway in the gentle breeze,
Nature’s art with perfect ease.
A tapestry of frost and light,
Illuminating the starry night.

In every shard a whisper lies,
Echoes of the winter skies.
A dreamscape formed of icy sheen,
In this world, we find the serene.

So let us dance in this frozen scene,
Chasing shadows, bright and keen.
For in the chill, our hopes will bloom,
In icicle dreams, dispelling gloom.

Celestial Chill

Stars unfurl in the night's deep blue,
A cosmic veil, a silent hue.
Whispers of frost dance on the breeze,
Under the gaze of ancient trees.

The moonlight spills on a glistening lake,
Reflecting dreams that softly wake.
Each breath of air, a frosty kiss,
In celestial chill, we find our bliss.

Where shadows shift and whispers soar,
In the heart of night, we yearn for more.
The heavens bend, the earth holds still,
Awakening magic, a snowy thrill.

Travel far on this silver tide,
With starlit wishes as our guide.
Through winter's charms, we seek the light,
In celestial chill, the world feels right.

So lift your gaze and take a chance,
Let your spirit waltz and dance.
For in this icy, wondrous space,
We find the warmth of love's embrace.

Silver Shroud

Wrapped in a cloak of shimmering white,
The world lies still, a tranquil sight.
Fields of snow, vast and deep,
In silver shroud, the earth does sleep.

Frosty whispers weave through the night,
Dreams take shape in the pale moonlight.
Each step is quiet, a soft caress,
The magic lies in this stillness blessed.

Trees stand tall with limbs adorned,
In crystal beauty, they are transformed.
A landscape painted with nature's brush,
In the silver shroud, there is no rush.

Embrace the chill; let your heart roam,
In winter's arms, we find our home.
With every flake that reaches the ground,
In whispered peace, our joy is found.

So linger on, in the frosty air,
For every moment, hold it dear.
In silver shroud, the world unfolds,
A timeless grace that never grows old.

Silent Radiance

In the hush of night so deep,
Stars awaken, secrets keep.
Whispers float on silver streams,
Wrapped in soft, celestial dreams.

Moonlight dances on the trees,
Casting shadows, gentle breeze.
Quiet moments, pure delight,
Silent radiance, endless light.

Thoughts adrift, time stands still,
Embraced by the cosmos' will.
Each heartbeat syncs with the glow,
Silent paths we come to know.

In the stillness, we confess,
Nature's beauty, nothing less.
Hearts entwined in tranquil grace,
Silent radiance, our embrace.

Dreams unfold beneath the sky,
Echoed wishes, soft and shy.
In the twilight, hopes ignite,
Guided by the silent light.

Ethereal Glow of Frostbite

Beneath the moon's tender gaze,
Frost patterns in a silvery haze.
Branches shimmer, a crystal treat,
In winter's grasp, the world feels sweet.

Whispers of an icy song,
Nature's beauty, vast and strong.
Every breath, a mystic dance,
Ethereal glow, a fleeting chance.

Footprints left on fresh, white snow,
Tell a tale of warmth and glow.
In the chill, hearts slowly thaw,
Ethereal light, nature’s law.

Colors muted, but still bright,
Under stars that paint the night.
Frostbite kisses, tender, shy,
Ethereal glow, see it fly.

In the cold, spirits unite,
Crafting dreams in soft moonlight.
Every moment crystal clear,
Ethereal glow, forever near.

Illuminated Dreams

In a realm of wish and wonder,
Dreams take flight, like rolling thunder.
Stars align in perfect streams,
Guiding us through illuminated dreams.

Tales of hope in shadows spun,
Where the light eclipses none.
Awake or sleep, we find our way,
In the glow of night and day.

With every heartbeat, visions grow,
Illuminated whispers flow.
Paths of light, we dare to chase,
In the warmth of this embrace.

Boundless skies and open seas,
Setting spirits free with ease.
Breathless moments, woven seams,
Life unfolds in illuminated dreams.

Through the night, we journey forth,
Treading paths of joy and worth.
With each step, our heart redeems,
In the magic of our dreams.

Hues of Cold Serenity

In twilight's grip, the world transforms,
Hues of gray where silence warms.
Each color whispers tales of peace,
In cold serenity, all troubles cease.

Soft blue skies, a fading light,
Holding shadows, bidding night.
Gentle breezes weave through trees,
Nature's canvas, soft as these.

Fields of frost with silver crowns,
Calmness deepens, echoes drown.
In stillness, hearts begin to soar,
In hues of calm, we crave for more.

Peeking stars in darkened seas,
Guiding dreams on gentle breeze.
Cold serenity, a silent song,
In this beauty, we belong.

Wrapped in warmth from afar,
In the night, we find our star.
Embracing peace like gentle streams,
Lost in hues of cold serene dreams.

Shards of Tranquility

Amidst the gentle breeze so light,
Whispers of calm in the fading night.
Stars above start to softly gleam,
In silence, we drift in a fragile dream.

Ripples of water mirror the sky,
Reflecting the peace as moments fly.
Nature's embrace, a soothing balm,
In this stillness, we find our calm.

Petals fall with a graceful ease,
Carried away by the evening's tease.
The world slows down, heartbeats blend,
In shards of tranquility, we transcend.

Crisp air wraps around like a shawl,
Under the spell, we surrender all.
In this space, worries fade away,
Carved in peace, we linger and stay.

Time drips slowly, a tranquil stream,
Holding our breath in a fleeting dream.
Each moment whispers, soft and light,
Forever held in this tranquil night.

Moonlit Echoes

Softly the moon begins to rise,
Casting silver down from the skies.
Whispers of night dance through the trees,
Echoes of dreams carried on the breeze.

Shadows flicker and gently sway,
A symphony sung by night's ballet.
The world transforms in luminescent grace,
Lost in the charm of this bewitching place.

Stars twinkle like laughter above,
Filling the night with a deep, sweet love.
Every echo brings stories anew,
Whispers of heartbeats and longing too.

In moonlit glow, secrets blend,
Where every night feels like no end.
Floating amidst this celestial glow,
In the echoes of dreams, together we flow.

As dawn approaches, shadows fade,
But the heart knows where memories laid.
Moonlit echoes, forever we hold,
In the tapestry of night, stories untold.

Aurora's Memory

Dancing colors ignite the dawn,
Painting the night as shadows yawn.
Whispers of light across the sky,
In the aurora, our spirits fly.

Violet hues blend with shades of gold,
A wondrous tale quietly told.
Each flicker holds the warmth of dreams,
In this canvas, everything gleams.

The chill of night softly retreating,
In the glow of morning, hearts are beating.
Nature's brush with splendor we see,
In every stroke, a memory free.

As colors meld in a joyous spree,
A reminder of what’s meant to be.
In the embrace of each fleeting ray,
Aurora's memory guides the way.

When the sun rises, whispers stay,
In the heart, they'll never stray.
A dance of colors written high,
In aurora's embrace, together we fly.

Glistening Veils

Morning dew on a gentle web,
Nature's lace where dreams ebb.
Each droplet shines like a hidden star,
Glistening veils, both near and far.

Soft whispers ride on the dawn's light,
Painting the world in colors so bright.
Sunrise kisses, a tender caress,
In each beam, a moment to bless.

The trees sway with a rhythmic grace,
Carrying stories through this sacred space.
Underneath the glistening veil,
Time stands still, we gently sail.

Nature speaks in a soft refrain,
In every sigh, a sweet, sweet gain.
Beneath the surface, beauty hides,
In glistening veils, the spirit abides.

Each glance reveals the world anew,
An invitation to wander through.
In sparkling light, we bask and dwell,
Wrapped in the magic of glistening veil.

Chasing the Pale Sun

In dawn's embrace, we start our race,
With shadows long, we'll find our place.
The whispers of light begin to play,
As dreams awaken with the day.

We dash through fields of golden hue,
With laughter bright, and skies of blue.
The sun, though pale, guides our flight,
A dance of joys, a pure delight.

Through valleys deep and mountains high,
We chase the sun that paints the sky.
With every step, our spirits rise,
In search of warmth, beneath the skies.

So let the world around us spin,
We'll chase the light that draws us in.
With hearts aglow and hands entwined,
Together, free, our fates aligned.

Nurtured by the Cold

In winter's grasp, we find our soul,
The frost that bites, it makes us whole.
Each breath like steam, in icy air,
A chill that humbles, a beauty rare.

The snowflakes dance, they twirl and glide,
A silent song, nature's guide.
In stillness deep, we learn to see,
The quiet strength in harmony.

Beneath the stars, the world in peace,
In frigid nights, our worries cease.
We gather close, our warmth a fire,
In frozen realms, we find desire.

Though cold may bite, it's love that warms,
In every storm, through every harm.
Together strong, we face the freeze,
In bonds of trust, our spirits ease.

Celestial Sprinkles

As night descends, a canvas blooms,
With stars like gems in velvet rooms.
Each twinkle tells a tale untold,
Of cosmic dreams and hearts of gold.

We gaze above, in wonder bound,
The universe whispers, a soothing sound.
With constellations tracing lines,
In starlit night, our spirit shines.

The moon, a guardian, whispers low,
In silver beams, our wishes grow.
As comets race and planets spin,
In celestial dances, we begin.

A sprinkle here, a splash of light,
In dreams we weave, the world feels right.
Each star a wish, a beacon bright,
We chase the magic of the night.

Twilight's Embrace

In twilight's hush, the world slows down,
A gentle fade, the day’s soft crown.
With hues of orange, pink, and gray,
We find our peace at the close of day.

The whispers cool as shadows blend,
In fading light, our hearts ascend.
With every breath, the stillness grows,
In twilight’s arms, the beauty shows.

Beneath the sky, our worries cease,
In this embrace, we find our peace.
The stars awaken, one by one,
In twilight’s glow, our dreams have spun.

So linger here, in this soft glow,
As day bids adieu, and night takes hold.
With every heartbeat, love will trace,
Eternal moments in twilight’s embrace.

Glints of Serenity at Dusk

Soft whispers float in the evening air,
Colors blend, a gentle flare.
Golden hues kiss the sky,
As day bids its sweet goodbye.

Silent shadows start to creep,
Nature wraps the world in sleep.
Stars awaken, one by one,
A tranquil peace has just begun.

The breeze carries stories old,
Of dreams and hopes yet untold.
Moonlight dances on the lake,
A soothing charm, for night's sake.

In this moment, time stands still,
Hearts are light, as spirits thrill.
With every glint of fading light,
We find our souls, taking flight.

As darkness falls, we gather close,
In whispered thoughts, we softly boast.
Together here, we share our trust,
In glints of serenity, we must.

Cold Sun's Fading Memory

Beneath the chill of autumn's breath,
The sun retreats, a hint of death.
Frosty whispers taint the morn,
As pale light starts to be reborn.

Shadows stretch on amber ground,
Where once warm rays danced all around.
Frigid air bites through the day,
Leaving echoes where warmth would play.

Memory of sunlight fades slow,
In twilight's grasp, it starts to go.
Yet in the chill, a beauty lies,
In silvered frost and painted skies.

Through barren branches, the cold winds sigh,
Melancholy notes, a soft goodbye.
Yet still, the heart can find some glow,
In the starkness of winter's show.

As night descends, a new calm reigns,
In the silence, peace remains.
With the sun's fading memory,
We hold onto what used to be.

Threads of Silvery Haze

In the morning, mist does weave,
A tapestry that bids us leave.
Threads of silver touch the ground,
In fog's embrace, peace can be found.

With every step, the world feels new,
Each breath taken, a stitch in blue.
Nature's canvas, soft and bright,
Inviting hearts to share its light.

The silence sings a gentle tune,
Underneath the watchful moon.
Moonlit paths, like dreams in chase,
Guide our wanderings through this space.

Each glimmer wraps us in its lace,
A dance of fog, a slow embrace.
In this moment, fears unwind,
And all is well, and all is kind.

As the day breaks, the haze grows thin,
But memories linger, deep within.
For in the threads of silvery haze,
We find our peace in quiet ways.

Echoes of a Pale Sun

In the morning light, shadows play,
Whispers of dreams fade away.
Golden hues touch the frost,
Remnants of warmth, nearly lost.

Clouds drift like thoughts in the sky,
Hiding the sun, a soft sigh.
Echoes linger, sweet yet faint,
A reminder of what was quaint.

Beneath the trees, silence stands,
Cradled softly in nature's hands.
Glimmers of hope in the dark,
Nature's song leaves its mark.

Time flows like a gentle stream,
Painted in whispers, a fleeting dream.
The pale sun hugs the earth tight,
Awaiting the promise of night.

Reach for the warmth, feel the grace,
In this luminous, quiet space.
Echoing tales of days gone by,
Beneath the vast and open sky.

Serenade of Ice

Frozen whispers fill the air,
A crystal melody everywhere.
Beneath the stars, shadows glide,
In winter's arms, we quietly bide.

The moonlight casts a silken glow,
On icy paths where soft winds blow.
Each flake a note, pure and clear,
Singing softly for all to hear.

Branches bowed with frosty lace,
Nature's beauty, a tender embrace.
Every breath, a fleeting sigh,
In this serene, enchanted sky.

As the night drapes its cool veil,
Stories of old begin to sail.
A serenade of frozen grace,
Whirls around in this sacred space.

Awakening dreams in the still,
Hopes wrapped tightly, a quiet thrill.
In the chill, warmth can be found,
In the hush, love's echoes abound.

Gleaming Heaven

In the dawn, the colors blend,
A canvas stretched without an end.
Stars retreat, their glow still bright,
Making way for morning light.

Whispers of gold, a gentle sweep,
Over valleys where shadows creep.
Promises linger in the shade,
As nature's beauty is displayed.

Clouds dance lightly, joy ignites,
Painting skies in wondrous heights.
With every heartbeat, the world spins,
Gleaming heaven as the day begins.

Fields of green stretch far and wide,
Cradling dreams where hopes reside.
All around, the beauty's clear,
In this moment, we draw near.

As daylight whispers sweet refrain,
Worries fade, like soft, warm rain.
Gleaming heaven, bright and true,
Cradles the heart, renews the view.

Radiant Stillness

In the quiet of twilight's embrace,
Time slows down in this sacred space.
Softly glowing, the world sighs,
Underneath expansive skies.

The hush of night brings peace untold,
While stars emerge, bright and bold.
Each flicker tells a story old,
Of dreams and wishes, softly scrolled.

Leaves rustle like a gentle tune,
A serenade beneath the moon.
Radiant stillness fills the air,
Whispers of blessings everywhere.

In the dark, a warmth ignites,
Illuminating hidden sights.
Reflections dance on the stream's face,
In radiant stillness, we find our place.

Time holds its breath, a moment's grace,
In every heartbeat, love's embrace.
All is calm, and yet it swells,
In the quiet, a story tells.

Echoes Beneath the Snow

With softest whispers, snowflakes fall,
Covering the world, blanketing all.
Silent echoes linger, void of sound,
Nature's hush, where peace is found.

Branches bow low, under winter’s weight,
Stillness surrounds, as dreams await.
Footsteps muffled on the cold, white ground,
In this silence, comfort is found.

Shadows dance under pale moonlight,
An ethereal glow graces the night.
Memories flicker, like stars on high,
Whispers of winter, time wandering by.

The world in slumber, wrapped in a shroud,
Each breath of frost felt, yet no crowds.
In tranquil beauty, the heart can grow,
Finding solace, echoes beneath the snow.

Celestial Chill

Stars shimmer brightly in the midnight sky,
A tapestry woven, where dreams lie.
The universe whispers, secrets untold,
Wrapped in a chill, as the night unfolds.

Frost kisses the ground, a delicate lace,
Each breath a mist in this wondrous space.
Celestial wonders, dancing above,
Silence enfolds like a winter love.

Constellations twinkle, guiding the way,
Carving paths through the dark, they sway.
In this vast cosmos, we find our place,
A celestial chill, a warm embrace.

Time drifts gently in the night's embrace,
Fleeting moments in this sacred space.
Hearts beat softly, under starry arcs,
Connecting souls in the whispers of sparks.

Beneath the chill, the fire within glows,
In the dance of the sun and moon's throes.
Celestial chill, a blanket of light,
Guiding us forth into the night.

Dappled Light in Gray

Morning breaks with a muted hue,
Gray clouds parting, revealing the blue.
Light dapples softly through branches bare,
A gentle reminder of beauty rare.

Shadows play on an earthen floor,
Echoes of laughter, now heard no more.
Nature hums in a quiet refrain,
Each note a whisper, both joy and pain.

In the stillness, life stirs awake,
Promises linger in every mistake.
Dappled light dances, a fleeting embrace,
Caressing the heart in this sacred space.

Time moves slowly; the world holds its breath,
Each moment a gift, a dance with death.
Color emerges, softening the day,
In dappled light, shadows gently sway.

As twilight descends in shades of gray,
The day bids farewell, drifting away.
Yet hope remains in each gentle ray,
In dappled light, we find our way.

Fragile Glare

A fragile glare breaks the morning mist,
Kissing the world, a tender tryst.
Light spills softly over fields so wide,
In its embrace, shadows bide.

Moments glisten, like dew on grass,
Glimmers of hope, as seasons pass.
In fragile gleams, life's beauty sings,
An ethereal light that softly clings.

With every heartbeat, a flicker of grace,
Guiding our way through this sacred space.
Each glow a promise that time does share,
In the softest touch of fragile glare.

The sun dips low, painting skies anew,
In hues of orange, and shades of blue.
Evening whispers as stars appear,
Life goes on in the quiet sphere.

In the twilight glow, we find our place,
Footprints left on this timeless base.
In every heartbeat, every prayer,
We cherish the beauty of fragile glare.

Ember Glints on the Edge

Flickering light in shadows dance,
Whispers of warmth in twilight's glance.
The fire's breath stirs memories near,
Embers glow softly, erasing fear.

Crimson sparks leap to the night,
Dancing with shadows, a delicate sight.
In the silence, stories unfold,
Each glint a heartbeat, tender and bold.

Night wraps the world in a deep embrace,
While embers spark dreams in open space.
The edge of darkness, a canvas wide,
With every flicker, spirits abide.

Moments linger, the past awakes,
Glints of ember that time forsakes.
In heartbeats shared, the warmth will stay,
Guiding lost souls along the way.

As dawn approaches, shadows wane,
Yet in the heart, embers remain.
Glowing softly in every breath,
Life thrives on, defying death.

Moonlit Pathways

Silver beams dance on the ground,
In stillness, magic can be found.
Through winding trails of whispered dreams,
The moonlight glimmers, softly gleams.

Phantom shadows, they softly glide,
Evening whispers, no need to hide.
Each step taken in gentle grace,
Guided by the moon's warm embrace.

The night calls forth the heart's delight,
Under stars, everything feels right.
Lost in wonder, we wander deep,
Where secrets of the night we keep.

As branches sway and breezes play,
Moonlit pathways lead the way.
With each breath, the world anew,
In silver light, dreams come true.

With dawn’s approach, the magic fades,
Yet in our hearts, the glow cascades.
A journey marked by night's sweet sighs,
Moonlit pathways never die.

Gleaming Snowflakes

Softly falling from skies so gray,
Gleaming snowflakes, a dance at play.
Whirls of white, a silent song,
In winter's arms, we all belong.

Each flake unique, a work of art,
Gentle as love, it touches the heart.
Frozen whispers on winter's breath,
In the stillness, they conquer death.

A blanket soft on the earth below,
Covering all with a sparkling glow.
Children laugh with joy untold,
As gleaming snowflakes shape the cold.

In the hush of night, a tranquil peace,
Gleaming snowflakes bring sweet release.
Every shimmer tells a tale,
Of winter nights and a snow-white veil.

As morning breaks, the sun will rise,
Melting magic beneath the skies.
Yet in our hearts, they will remain,
Gleaming snowflakes, a soft refrain.

Crystalline Mirage

A shimmer of light on shifting sands,
Where dreams dissolve in fated hands.
Crystalline visions dance and sway,
In the mirror of the fading day.

Illusions rise with the shifting breeze,
Whispers of tales that wander with ease.
Glimmers wrap around the mind,
Shadows of thoughts, intertwined.

As twilight falls, the colors blend,
Mirages beckon, and echoes send.
Each breath of promise, a fleeting sight,
In crystalline whispers, lost in the night.

A world unfolding, both near and far,
Dancing beneath the evening star.
With every heartbeat, visions merge,
Crystalline mirage, an endless surge.

Yet morning light will break the spell,
Revealing truths we know so well.
In every shimmer, a story stays,
Crystalline mirage, lost sunlit rays.

Crystal Veil of Solstice

Beneath the crystal sky, so bright,
The solstice whispers through the night.
Stars align with ancient grace,
Time wraps softly in their embrace.

Frosted branches, glimmering white,
Shimmering dreams take flight tonight.
A canvas painted, silver and blue,
Nature's magic, fresh and new.

Echoes of laughter fill the air,
As the world pauses, blissful and rare.
In moments fleeting, we find our place,
Freed by the warmth of love’s embrace.

With each heartbeat, rhythms blend,
In quiet solace, we transcend.
The crystal veil, our hearts entwined,
In the solstice glow, at peace we find.

As dawn awakens, colors unfold,
Stories of winter gently told.
The cycle turns, yet here we stand,
Together, united, hand in hand.

Radiant Echoes of Stillness

In the stillness, whispers flow,
Radiant echoes start to grow.
Leaves dance softly in the breeze,
Carving moments with such ease.

Golden sunlight filters down,
Beneath the branches, wearing a crown.
Nature's choir begins to sing,
In harmony, the earth takes wing.

Rippling waters, crystal clear,
Each gentle wave a tale we hear.
Reflections shimmer, truth bestowed,
In the silence, love's abode.

Time stands still, fate intertwines,
With every heartbeat, our soul aligns.
In the glow of the waning light,
We find solace, pure delight.

As shadows stretch, the day must close,
But in our hearts, the warmth still glows.
Radiant echoes of the day,
Forever linger, come what may.

Glistening in the Gloom

Beneath a blanket, soft and gray,
The world ignites in dim display.
Glistening whispers, shadows talk,
In twilight's warmth, we softly walk.

Stars peek out, a hidden song,
Guiding us where we belong.
The moonlight dances on the ground,
In this quiet, magic is found.

Through the fog, our spirits soar,
In the stillness, we seek more.
Glistening dreams in the deep night,
Awakening beauty, pure and bright.

Hands entwined in the evening air,
Together we chase away despair.
In the gloom, our hopes ignite,
Illuminated by love's light.

As dawn approaches, shadows fade,
In the soft glow, our hearts are made.
Glistening moments, tenderly shared,
In the gloom, we were unprepared.

Threads of Sun in Frost

In the frosty morning's glow,
Threads of sun begin to show.
Each glimmer tells a tale untold,
In nature's weave, a sight to behold.

Winter’s chill gives way to warmth,
As daylight dances, bright and swarth.
With sparkling jewels on every tree,
A tapestry of life, wild and free.

The whispers of the dawn arise,
A gentle peace beneath the skies.
With every beam, the world awakes,
In the stillness, magic breaks.

Threads of hope in the icy breath,
A promise of renewal after death.
In nature's arms, we find our worth,
Beneath the frost, a vibrant earth.

With each moment, we softly tread,
In the light, where dreams are fed.
Threads of sun, a bright embrace,
In frost and warmth, we find our place.

Frosted Lullabies

Whispers of the cold night,
Gentle snowflakes dance and sway.
Crystalline dreams take flight,
In winter's soft embrace, they lay.

Stars twinkle in the dark,
Creating a serene display.
Wrapped in warmth, spark by spark,
The world is still, in soft decay.

Moonlight paints the silent ground,
A silver glow on nature's bloom.
Where peace and quiet can be found,
In frosted nights, a gentle room.

The air is crisp, alive with sighs,
Echoes of a world at rest.
Each breath a soft, sweet reprise,
Lullabies of winter's best.

With every flake, a story spun,
In the hush of the frozen night.
Frosted lullabies softly run,
Cradling dreams till morning light.

Palescent Skies

Palescent hues of dawn arise,
As night retreats in tender grace.
Morning whispers through the skies,
A canvas bright, a warm embrace.

Clouds drift like thoughts, so light,
Brushing past the waking trees.
Colors blend, a soft delight,
Filling hearts with gentle ease.

Birds take flight in silent cheer,
Chasing rays of golden sun.
In their song, all doubts unclear,
A new day waits, a race begun.

The breeze carries tales untold,
Through fields where flowers bloom and sway.
Each moment precious, bright and bold,
In palescent skies, the world at play.

As shadows lengthen, sun will dip,
Cloaking earth in twilight's grace.
A lingering kiss on daylight's lip,
In palescent hues, we find our place.

Hazy Morning Wisp

A wisp of fog hangs in the air,
Morning shyly starts to glow.
Dreams linger, tender and rare,
In the warmth of the sun's soft show.

Branches wear a silver veil,
Swaying gently in quiet cheer.
Nature whispers, telling tales,
Of the night that drew so near.

Footsteps echoed on the path,
As shadows play on dewy grass.
Each step away from healing wrath,
Towards the light where moments pass.

The world awakens, pulses free,
Colors bloom from dusk's embrace.
Hazy whispers, a melody,
Inviting all to find their place.

As the sun lays claim to day,
Misty dreams begin to clear.
In the light, we choose to stay,
Lost in time’s embracing sphere.

Glinting Frost

Glinting frost on windowpane,
Whispering secrets of the night.
A crystalline world, beautifully plain,
Where dreams spark in the morning light.

Each blade of grass, a jewel rare,
Glistening under the sun's warm kiss.
Nature wrapped in a frosty layer,
A sparkling scene, a scene of bliss.

Breath hangs heavy in the cold air,
Clouds of warmth, a fleeting sight.
Embracing the chill, without a care,
Underneath this canvas bright.

Time moves slower, in this spell,
Each moment precious, pure and clear.
In the stillness, hearts can swell,
Finding joy in frosty cheer.

As the sun begins to rise,
Frost will fade, but not its song.
In the glinting warmth of skies,
We hold dear where we belong.

Glimmers on Snow

Gentle glimmers dance and play,
Underneath the bright sun's ray.
Each flake shines like a tiny star,
Whispers of winter from afar.

Footprints trace a tale untold,
In the depths of dreams so bold.
Silence wrapped in frosty air,
Nature's blanket, pure and rare.

A soft wind carries secrets old,
Veils of shimmering white unfold.
Trees adorned in crystal glow,
A frozen wonder, pure as snow.

As day fades into twilight's hue,
Colors blend from gold to blue.
The world glows in soft repose,
Embracing warmth that winter shows.

With every breath, the magic grows,
Underneath the moonlit prose.
In the stillness, hearts ignite,
Embracing dreams in winter's light.

Chasing Shadows in Hibernation

In the depths of winter's keep,
Silent whispers, secrets sleep.
Shadows linger, softly sway,
In the quiet, dreams at play.

Moonbeams dance upon the ground,
Chasing echoes, light and sound.
Nature’s hush, a soothing balm,
In the cold, the heart stays calm.

Frosted branches, pale and white,
Guard the secrets of the night.
While the world dreams, wrapped in snow,
Silent stories start to flow.

Beneath the surface, life awaits,
In the stillness, magic creates.
Chasing shadows, hearts align,
In the warmth of dreams divine.

As spring beckons, soft and near,
Awakened hearts shed winter's fear.
In the dance of light and shade,
Life begins, unafraid, unmade.

Candleflame in the Chill

A candle flickers, soft and low,
In the corner's gentle glow.
Against the chill of winter’s breath,
It whispers life, defying death.

Each flame a story, warm and bright,
Casting shadows, dancing light.
The room aglow with hope anew,
A refuge found in pale and blue.

Warmth surrounds the hearts that gather,
In the stillness, laughter gathers.
Embers crackle, spirits soar,
In the night, we seek for more.

Outside the world is cold and grim,
Inside, dreams dance on a whim.
Candleflame, a cherished friend,
Guiding souls until the end.

As the night gives way to dawn,
The flames flicker, gently drawn.
Yet in our hearts, the warmth will stay,
A beacon bright, come what may.

Silver Whispers of Twilight

Twilight drapes a silver veil,
Painting skies with softest pale.
Whispers echo through the trees,
As daylight bows to evening's tease.

Stars awaken, bold and bright,
Piercing through the cloak of night.
Each twinkling light, a secret shared,
In the silence, souls are bared.

The moon ascends, a watchful eye,
Cloaked in velvet, calm and shy.
Gentle shadows stretch and twine,
In the embrace of dusk, we dine.

Cool breezes rustle leaves around,
Nature whispers without sound.
In twilight’s grace, we chance to roam,
Finding peace so far from home.

As darkness falls, we know it’s true,
In silver whispers, dreams renew.
A moment held, in time's sweet clasp,
Twilight’s breath, a tender gasp.

Embers of the Frostbitten Dawn

In the stillness, shadows play,
Whispers of night gently sway.
Crimson hues meet icy breath,
Life unfolds beyond sweet death.

A chill lingers on each branch,
Silent stories in a trance.
The sun peeks, a timid flame,
Awakening all the same.

Frost-kissed petals, soft as sighs,
Reflecting truth in winter's guise.
A dance of warmth, a tender spark,
Illuminating the hidden dark.

As daylight breaks the frozen night,
Embers glow with pure delight.
The world transforms, anew begins,
In the light where hope still spins.

With every breath, new stories grow,
In the dawning's tender glow.
Frostbitten dreams take flight and soar,
In this moment, forevermore.

The Calm Before the Thaw

Quiet hangs in the crisp air,
Nature waits, a secret flare.
Beneath the surface, whispers creep,
Life is stirring from its sleep.

Branches bare, yet full of grace,
Time stands still in this space.
The earth holds its breath with pride,
In this calm, dreams bide.

Hope flickers like candlelight,
Promising warmth beyond the night.
Softly come the gentle rains,
Melting all the winter's chains.

Birds awaken, songs take flight,
Painting skies with pure delight.
A world reborn from frozen fears,
As spring approaches, it draws near.

The calm before the great reveal,
Where life, once more, begins to heal.
In this pause, we sense the change,
Nature's art, intricately strange.

Figments of Candlelight

Shadows dance on the wall,
Echoes of a distant call.
Flickering dreams, soft and bright,
Guiding souls through the night.

Candles whisper tales untold,
In the darkness, brave and bold.
Each flame a heart, a fervent wish,
As reality begins to swish.

The room transforms, a golden glow,
Imagined worlds begin to flow.
Every flicker, a story spun,
In candlelight, we find our fun.

Moments captured in the light,
Laughter shared, a pure delight.
In this space, our hearts ignite,
Figments born of candlelight.

As shadows blend with soft embrace,
We lose ourselves, find our place.
In this glow, love's shadows play,
Guiding us through night and day.

Glimmers in the Gloom

Amidst the dark, a spark will rise,
A glimmer found in quiet sighs.
Faint light dances on the ground,
In the gloom, hope can be found.

Whispers of dawn slip through the night,
Each glimmer, a promise, a guiding light.
Stars shine bright, tales in their glow,
Unspoken words begin to flow.

In the silence, courage stirs,
Brave souls chase away the blurs.
With every heartbeat, dreams align,
In shadows, joys intertwine.

The journey through the dark and deep,
Is adorned with hope we keep.
Each step taken, a light we choose,
Glimmers in the gloom we use.

Hand in hand, we face the night,
Finding strength in every plight.
In darkness, we shall bravely zoom,
Embracing glimmers in the gloom.

Subtle Illuminations

In the quiet of the night,
Stars weave tales of old,
A gentle light ignites,
Whispers of secrets unfold.

Moonbeams cast their glow,
On paths where dreams reside,
Guiding hearts to flow,
Where hopes and fears collide.

Shadows dance with glee,
In the soft, silken air,
Echoes roam so free,
A magic found rare.

Each flicker tells a tale,
Of journeys yet untold,
Where starlit ships set sail,
In the arms of the bold.

Underneath the vast sky,
We gather moments bright,
Together we will fly,
In subtle illuminations of light.

Radiant Whisper of the Frost

On a canvas of white,
The frost gently creeps,
Whispers in the light,
Where silence softly sleeps.

Each flake tells a tale,
Of winter's breath so sweet,
Time begins to pale,
As chill and warmth meet.

Beneath the icy glaze,
Fields shimmer and shine,
In a delicate haze,
Nature's art divine.

With each frosty dawn,
A sparkle in the air,
Dreams shall be reborn,
In moments truly rare.

Softly now we tread,
On this icy ground,
Where whispers have led,
In frost, peace is found.

Sparkling Dawn

With the break of day,
The sky blushes bright,
Golden rays that play,
Chasing off the night.

Birds begin to sing,
A chorus of hope,
Life's refreshing spring,
In colors that cope.

Dewdrops gleam like stars,
Adorning each leaf,
The world free of scars,
Embracing relief.

Every footstep glows,
On this pristine path,
Where the warmth now flows,
In nature's sweet bath.

Hearts awaken new,
With the morning's call,
Embracing the view,
Of dawn's sparkling thrall.

Ineffable Glow

In the silence of dusk,
A light begins to swell,
Beyond any husk,
Where stories dwell.

Veils of twilight fall,
Kissing the weary ground,
In shadows that call,
Echoes are profound.

Each moment we share,
Is woven in the night,
In whispers of air,
A tapestry of light.

Hearts beat in rhythm,
With stars in their flight,
A glow that is given,
To guide through the night.

Endless and aglow,
Beyond what we know,
In the vast, surreal,
Lies the ineffable glow.

Shimmering Frost on Pine

Beneath the boughs, the cold does creep,
Crystals whisper in the deep.
Nature's shimmer, soft and bright,
Guides the stars in silent flight.

Each needle dressed in icy lace,
Glistening softly, a sweet embrace.
Morning's breath, a gentle sigh,
Awakens dreams as shadows fly.

In the hush of dawn's first light,
The frosted world feels soft and right.
A whispered spell of winter's grace,
Enfolds all in a warm embrace.

Branches bow with heavy weights,
Nature pauses, patiently waits.
The glimmering frost, a fleeting guest,
Tells the tales of winter's rest.

When nightfall comes, the chill takes hold,
Stars dance brightly, stories told.
Underneath the blanket white,
The world sleeps soundly, wrapped tight.

Flickering Flame against the Chill

In the hearth, a fire burns bright,
Casting warmth into the night.
Dancing flames in wild ballet,
Chasing all the cold away.

Each crackle sings a tale of old,
Of cozy nights and hearts consoled.
The flickering light, a guiding star,
Fends off shadows, near and far.

Gathered close, we share our dreams,
In the glow, the laughter beams.
Hands are warmed, spirits rise,
As the night reveals its skies.

Outside, the frost begins to creep,
While inside, memories we keep.
The flame whispers of hope and cheer,
A refuge found, right here, right here.

So let the cold winds howl and call,
Within these walls, we have it all.
A flickering flame, the heart's delight,
Guides us through the longest night.

Beneath the Winter's Gaze

Underneath the silent snow,
Nature sleeps, a gentle glow.
Whispers flow through bitter air,
Secrets shared with winter's care.

Trees stand tall, their branches bare,
Guardians of the frigid air.
Beneath the stars, the earth holds still,
Awaiting spring, with silent thrill.

Footprints press upon the ground,
Echoes of the joy we've found.
Breath like smoke in the frosty night,
Dreams take flight, hearts feel light.

The moon peeks through the clouds above,
Blanketing all in beams of love.
In winter's grasp, we find our place,
Awake, alive in nature's grace.

Beneath the gaze of winter's eye,
We weave our dreams, our hopes, our sighs.
In stillness, life begins anew,
A promise whispered, fresh and true.

Luminous Hush of December

Snowflakes twirl in graceful dance,
Each a light, a fleeting chance.
In the air, a magic stirs,
Wrapped around the whispered purrs.

The world adorned in white, so pure,
A tranquil calm, a soft allure.
In December's hush, we find peace,
As time slows down, and worries cease.

Beneath the sky, a canvas wide,
Frosted breath, a gentle guide.
Children play, their laughter bright,
In the radiant glow of fading light.

Homes aglow with warm embrace,
Fires crackle in every space.
Hearts entwined in love's sweet thread,
Gathered close, where fears are shed.

So let the stars above ignite,
The dreams we share on winter's night.
In the luminous hush we remain,
Bound together, through joy and pain.

Ethereal Glow

In the twilight's soft embrace,
Stars awaken, light the space.
Moonlight dances on the stream,
Whispers secrets, like a dream.

Gentle breezes touch the trees,
Carrying scents upon the freeze.
Nature's song, a lullaby,
Elysian hues that lift us high.

Clouds adorned in silver lace,
Bathe the world in their grace.
Every shadow starts to bloom,
Wrapped in magic, dispelling gloom.

Moments linger, time stands still,
Hearts entwined by fate’s sweet will.
Underneath this celestial show,
We find peace in the glow.

A canvas painted night’s caress,
In this realm, we find our rest.
Together, we'll forever stay,
In the night that fades away.

Whispering Shadows

In the twilight's gentle hush,
Shadows dance in a soft rush.
Faint whispers glide on the breeze,
Secrets hidden in the trees.

Moonlight weaves a silver thread,
Guiding dreams from hearts long fed.
Echoes linger, faint and low,
As night’s magic starts to flow.

Footsteps light on paths unseen,
Where the world remains serene.
Each shadow tells a story old,
In the dark, mysteries unfold.

Branches sway with ancient grace,
Holding time in sweet embrace.
Stars peek through the velvet veil,
Chasing the night’s secret tale.

In this realm where silence reigns,
Whispering shadows shed their chains.
In the dark, together we roam,
Finding solace, feeling home.

Frosted Dawn

Morning breaks with icy breath,
Nature glimmers, whispers death.
Frosty patterns quilt the ground,
In the stillness, peace is found.

The sun rises, paint anew,
Gold and silver start to strew.
Gentle rays warm winter's heart,
Giving life a fresh new start.

Breath of life in winter’s chill,
Every moment, hearts can fill.
Deeper still, the silence grows,
Trust the beauty that it shows.

Softly, the world comes alive,
Nature’s wonders start to thrive.
Frosted edges gleam and shine,
In this dawn, we feel divine.

With each breath, we embrace hope,
In the stillness, learn to cope.
Frosted dawns bring joy to see,
Whispers of sweet harmony.

Glistening Silence

In the depth of glistening night,
Silence wraps the world so tight.
Stars like diamonds softly gleam,
In this hush, we dare to dream.

Waves of calm caress our souls,
Quiet moments make us whole.
Every heartbeat sings a song,
In this silence, we belong.

Shadows play in silver light,
Every corner feels so right.
Echoes linger, soft and sweet,
In this stillness, love's heartbeat.

Softly breathed, the night unfolds,
Every secret gently holds.
Wrapped in light, we find our way,
In this silence, here we'll stay.

Glistening like the morning dew,
In these moments, calm and true.
Whispers shared, our spirits rise,
In glistening silence, light defies.

Twilight's Embrace

Shadows stretch across the land,
Whispers of night, in silence stand.
Stars begin to gently gleam,
Wrapped in dusk, we drift, it seems.

A soft breeze through branches sighs,
Painting colors in the skies.
The sun dips low on the horizon,
Embracing peace, when day is gone.

Voices fade into the dark,
Nature's lullaby, a gentle spark.
On this threshold of the night,
Hearts find solace in the light.

Fleeting moments, time stands still,
Each breath a gift, a whispered thrill.
In twilight's arms, we find our place,
Lost in dreams, in sweet embrace.

As starlight dances in the air,
We linger softly, without a care.
In the hush, our souls align,
In twilight's glow, your hand in mine.

Glacial Threads

Whispers of ice beneath the sky,
Crystal trails where shadows lie.
Nature's art, in stillness cast,
Frozen images from the past.

Mountains rise with a silent grace,
Holding secrets in their embrace.
Echoes of winter, unmarred and clear,
Stories of ages, we pause to hear.

Each flake that falls, a transient gift,
Caressing earth with a gentle drift.
Cold winds weave through the silent trees,
A symphony carried on the breeze.

Glistening patterns in moonlit nights,
Chasing shadows, chasing lights.
In the stillness, we find our thread,
Tales of frost in the silence spread.

Serenaded by the world's white song,
In glacial threads where hearts belong.
Winter's breath, a calming bond,
In icy realms, we wander fond.

Silent Luminescence

Through the dark, a glow appears,
Softly glowing, calming fears.
Hidden wonders, softly bright,
In the stillness of the night.

Light that dances on the streams,
Giving life to hidden dreams.
Every flicker, every ray,
Guides the lost along their way.

A quiet grace in every beam,
Moments captured in a dream.
Whispers of the unseen glow,
In their warmth, we come to know.

Stars above, like scattered seeds,
Planting hope within our needs.
Silent luminescence shines,
In the dark, your heart aligns.

As dawn approaches, colors blend,
Time to cherish, time to mend.
In light’s embrace, we find our stance,
Through silent paths, in life’s dance.

Morning's Whisper

First light breaks with gentle hands,
Chasing dreams across the lands.
Birds awaken, sweet notes rise,
Kissing night with soft goodbyes.

The sun spills gold on waking dew,
Painting skies in vibrant hue.
Nature yawns, and stretches wide,
As morning whispers, full of pride.

Each petal glistens, fresh and new,
A canvas bright where wonders grew.
In the hush, the world ignites,
With every heartbeat, pure delights.

Yet in the calm, a moment's pause,
Reflecting life's unending cause.
With every dawn, a chance to start,
Morning whispers to the heart.

Embrace the day with open arms,
Feel its warmth and endless charms.
In morning's light, let spirits soar,
In each new hour, discover more.

Translucent Chill

In the hush of evening's grace,
Whispers of the cold embrace,
Moonlight dances on the frost,
A fleeting warmth, forever lost.

Silent shadows drift and play,
As twilight bids the sun good day,
Branches sigh in icy breath,
Nature's touch, a subtle death.

Glimmers sparkle, crisp and bright,
Stars begin their watchful night,
The air, like glass, so pure and clear,
Each sigh drawn in, each word sincere.

Footsteps crunch on layers deep,
In this world where secrets sleep,
Captured in a moment's spell,
Translucent chill, a soft farewell.

Every glance a fleeting blush,
Every heartbeat starts to rush,
So we linger, hearts aligned,
In the chill, our warmth we find.

Evening's Icicle Glow

When dusk unfurls its velvet cloak,
A shimmer wraps the trees in smoke,
Icicles, like whispered dreams,
Hang gently where the starlight beams.

The world adorned in icy hues,
A canvas brushed with winter's blues,
In the distance, shadows creep,
Caressing silence, soft and deep.

Each breath released, a fleeting sonnet,
In evening's grasp, we find our font,
A glow that flickers, soft and low,
Guiding hearts in the evening's flow.

Through branches bare, the moonlight weaves,
A tale of frost among the leaves,
Together wrapped in night’s embrace,
Icicles glimmer, pure and chaste.

Time stands still as stars align,
In the space where hearts entwine,
Evening's glow, a gentle show,
Holding dreams in whispered flow.

Chilling Embrace

Beneath the weight of winter's breath,
A chilling grasp, a dance with death,
Yonder lies the frozen lake,
Where secrets stir and shadows wake.

The night unfolds its icy wings,
Against the hush, a silence clings,
A world wrapped tight in snowy white,
Enveloped by the tranquil night.

Each heartbeat echoes, loud and clear,
In the solitude, we hold dear,
A chilling embrace, so bittersweet,
Where time stands still and spirits meet.

Moonlight spills its silver hue,
Painting pathways fresh and new,
Hand in hand, we stroll along,
In chilling embrace, our hearts belong.

Through frigid air, our laughter rings,
A symphony the darkness brings,
As winter whispers, soft and low,
In chilling embrace, forever so.

Frosted Dawn

With the dawn, a world reborn,
Every branch with frost is adorned,
Sunlight glimmers on the snow,
Awakening all life below.

Shadows stretch across the ground,
In this beauty, peace is found,
Breath of winter, crisp and bright,
A canvas touched by morning light.

Birds begin their sweet refrain,
Nature whispers, soft as rain,
In the stillness, hope arise,
As frost-kissed morn greets azure skies.

Each petal gleams with icy dew,
Colors bloom in every hue,
Frosted dawn, a gentle sigh,
As daybreak paints the waking sky.

With every step, we leave a trace,
In the beauty of this place,
Frosted dawn, forever bright,
Guides us through the fading night.

Solitude Illuminated

In quiet woods I find my peace,
The gentle rustle, nature's lease.
Each whisper calls, a soft embrace,
In solitude, I find my place.

The sunlight filters through the trees,
A golden glow upon the leaves.
Each shadow dances, flickers bright,
In solitude, I find my light.

With every step upon the ground,
A world of beauty all around.
I walk the path, my spirit free,
In solitude, I truly see.

The heartbeats echo, slow and low,
In stillness, life begins to flow.
The silence sings, a soothing sound,
In solitude, my soul is found.

As daylight wanes and dusk draws near,
The stars appear, the skies are clear.
Serenity wraps me in the night,
In solitude, all feels just right.

Dappled Light in Frozen Boughs

In winter's grip, the world stands still,
The icy branches, white and chill.
Yet sunlight breaks through every frost,
A dance of light, at no great cost.

The dappled gleam on fallen snow,
A shimmering touch, a fleeting glow.
The frozen boughs, adorned with bright,
In winter's heart, a pure delight.

Each beam that kisses coldest air,
Transforms the scene, both bright and rare.
Nature's brush, with tender care,
Paints frosted dreams, a canvas fair.

Among the trees in silence deep,
I wander here, my thoughts I keep.
Dappled light dances through the grey,
Inviting warmth in cold decay.

As twilight falls, the colors blend,
A peaceful calm, the day's sweet end.
In frozen boughs, I find my peace,
Dappled light whispers of release.

Shining Through the Chill

Upon the path where cold winds blow,
The sunshine breaks, a warm hello.
Each ray that pierces through the frost,
A promise kept, never lost.

In chilly air, a breath so light,
Reminds me of the day’s delight.
As shadows play upon the ground,
Shining through the chill, joy is found.

With every step, the world awakes,
As sunlight dances, warmth it makes.
The frost retreats, the earth's embrace,
Shining through the chill, we find grace.

Together with the light, we roam,
In nature's arms, we make our home.
The cold may bite, but hearts are warm,
Shining through the chill, love's true form.

As day gives way to evening's tide,
The glow persists, it will not hide.
For in the dawn, we'll start anew,
Shining through the chill, I'll find you.

Aurora's Gentle Touch

In quiet night, the heavens glow,
An artist's brush begins to show.
With every hue, a dream unfolds,
Aurora's touch, a tale retold.

The skies ignite in vibrant dance,
Colors swirl, a cosmic romance.
Each flicker weaves a story bright,
With Aurora's gentle light.

Beneath the stars, I gaze in awe,
The beauty vast, without a flaw.
Nature's canvas spreads so wide,
Aurora's touch, our hearts collide.

As night gives way to morning's glow,
The promise of a new dawn flows.
The world awakens, fresh and new,
Aurora's touch, a gift so true.

In every heart, the magic stays,
A memory of those bright displays.
In silence held, our spirits soar,
Aurora's gentle touch, evermore.

Resplendent Haze of January

A frost-kissed dawn awakens slow,
With whispering winds in a soft glow.
Golden rays on white do play,
Painting warmth for the coldest day.

Trees draped in shimmering lace,
Breath of winter, a gentle grace.
Footprints trail on a glistening path,
Nature's beauty, a quiet laugh.

Beneath the surface, life lies still,
In the heart of frost, there’s a thrill.
Hope sleeps, wrapped in a crystal hue,
Awaiting the sun's embrace anew.

Clouds float by, a soft parade,
Casting shadows where dreams are made.
Every moment a fleeting dream,
An echo of winter's silver gleam.

As daylight fades, colors collide,
In twilight's arms, the world will bide.
Resplendent haze, soft and wide,
Winter's charm, our silent guide.

The Silence of Glinty Skies

Beneath the stars, the world holds breath,
In quiet moments, we find depth.
The moon whispers secrets of old,
Stories of times, in silver told.

A gentle breeze weaves through the night,
Carrying dreams, taking flight.
Each twinkle a wish from the heart,
In the stillness, we play our part.

Shadows dance on the velvet ground,
In the silence, a soothing sound.
Glistening orbs in a deep blue vault,
Nature's canvas, a pulsing jolt.

The chill of night wraps close and tight,
While stars shimmer in radiant light.
A celestial stage, endless and vast,
Moments of magic forever cast.

The silence sings of peace divine,
In the cosmos, our hearts align.
In every sigh, in every star,
The silence tells us who we are.

Light on the Edge of Winter

A soft glow lingers at sunset's edge,
Whispers of warmth on the frosty hedge.
The world bathes in hues of gold,
As day bows down, warmth unfolds.

Chill still clings to the fading light,
Yet sparkles dance with pure delight.
Nature breathes, a sigh of peace,
In every shade, worries cease.

Echoes of laughter float through the air,
In the golden hour, without a care.
Children play, their joy revealed,
As winter softens, hearts are healed.

The trees stand tall, draped in light,
Casting shadows of joyous height.
A fleeting moment, a precious gift,
As day and night in twilight shift.

With every ray that gently breaks,
Life awakens, the silence shakes.
Light on the edge, a promise near,
Whispers of spring that soon will cheer.

Shards of Daylight

Sunrise spills through a fractured sky,
Lighting the darkness with a soft sigh.
Golden shards of radiant beams,
Unraveling shadows, revealing dreams.

Each moment a gift, fragile and bright,
Breaking free from the grasp of night.
Morning's kiss, a tender embrace,
Awakens the world with gentle grace.

Leaves glisten with dew like diamonds clear,
Fresh beginnings that draw us near.
Every ray, a story to tell,
In the warmth, we begin to dwell.

Paths illuminated, colors unfold,
Whispers of life in the dawn’s gold.
Shards of daylight, a dance in the air,
Encouraging hearts to shed their despair.

The day unfurls like a vibrant flower,
Bathed in the light, we bloom, we tower.
With each breath, let the beauty blend,
Shards of daylight, our spirit mend.

Light's Gentle Embrace

Softly the dawn breaks, a whisper of grace,
Illuminating shadows, they dance in place.
Golden hues sprinkle the morning sky,
Nestled in warmth, as moments drift by.

Each beam that spills forth, a tender caress,
Chasing away night, in radiant dress.
Hopeful hearts open, like petals to sun,
In light's gentle embrace, we've only begun.

The world awakens, with laughter and cheer,
Every new day brings the promise that's clear.
With love's gentle touch, the soul is fulfilled,
In light's warm embrace, our dreams are instilled.

Frosty Reflections

A mirror of winter, glistening bright,
Patterns of ice weave through the night.
Trees stand adorned in shimmering white,
Nature's own canvas, a breathtaking sight.

Silent whispers carried by frigid air,
Footsteps are muffled, as if in a prayer.
Frozen lakes cradle, secrets untold,
In this frosty realm, all feelings unfold.

Reflections of stars twinkle above,
Blankets of frost, like kisses of love.
Time stands still in this wintry trance,
Each heartbeat echoes, as hearts dare to dance.

Hushed Sonnet of Winter

A hush blankets earth, soft and profound,
In winter’s embrace, where peace can be found.
Gentle flakes fall, a delicate hymn,
Nature's own symphony, quiet and dim.

Whispers of snowflakes, a whispering breeze,
Trees bow their heads in calm reveries.
Amongst the stillness, dreams drift and sway,
In hushed sonnets of winter, we find our way.

Candles flicker softly, casting a glow,
Inside the heart, the warmth begins to grow.
In the silence of night, the world feels alive,
In this hushed sonnet, our spirits revive.

Celestial Frost

Stars dust the night with a silvery sheen,
A canvas of frost, so magical and keen.
Whispers of heaven float down like a sigh,
In the chill of the dusk, where dreams softly lie.

Moonlight cascades, painting shadows below,
Embracing the earth in a delicate glow.
Waltzing with frost, the night begins to bloom,
In celestial realms, dispelling the gloom.

As dreams take flight on a cold winter's eve,
Wonders unfold, what the heart can conceive.
Celestial frost weaves a tale so divine,
In the night's gentle arms, our souls intertwine.

www.ingramcontent.com/pod-product-compliance
Ingram Content Group UK Ltd.
Pitfield, Milton Keynes, MK11 3LW, UK
UKHW031944151224
452382UK00006B/124

9 789916 794654